AUTHOR	Tellov
TRANSLATION	Cyrille Vollet, Susan Kanas
ILLUSTRATIONS	Susan Kanas, André Kanas
CORRECTIONS	Susanna Hsing, Nicky Wyles
DESIGN	Emmanuel Kormann

Tellov

Thirty poems
AT THE MARKET

© 2021, Tellov Tellov
Édition : BoD – Books on Demand,
12/14 rond-point des Champs-Élysées, 75008 Paris
Impression : BoD - Books on Demand, Norderstedt, Allemagne
ISBN: 9782322376315
Dépôt légal : Juin 2021

PREFACE

In 2018, I released a book called *L'Insoumis* and started to sell it at the market. This experience has been (and still is) rich in surprising events, meetings and rare moments.

Often, people are poetic without even realizing it. This is what I've tried to write about.

I have to say a special 'thank you' to Vincent. He was the first to welcome me at the market of Saint-Cyprien. He invited me to his stand to sell my books although we didn't know each other. I won't forget it.

Thank you to Carine, too, whom I met at Vincent's stand. She has supported me in many ways.

This book is not just my own. It's also Charley's book. She drew the illustrations for free, gave me one of her late husband's drawings of horses, and she spread the word across several continents. I'd like to dedicate this book to her, to Charley, the youthful old woman, my friend.

SAINTE-ALVÈRE MARKET

Today
A little girl made an ass of me
It happened so fast

My friend Pedro had accosted some passers-by
Saying
"Look at this young man
He's a poet
He wrote a novel in just one night
He's very talented
But you know his problem?
He's too shy…"

Hearing this
The little girl started laughing
Hidden behind her parents
She couldn't believe
A grown-up could be shy
And when she saw it was true
She teased
"Oh look, he's so shy!"

Her parents finally bought a book
They probably felt sorry for me

✶✶

AT THE END OF THE MARKET

We were loading hundreds of books
Into Vincent's truck
Carine was there too
She said she didn't understand poetry
I tried to explain what it meant to me

Then Vincent
Who was inside the truck
Storing books
Half drunk
Shouted
"What are you two talking about?"
I called back
"We're talking about poetry
Carine doesn't understand what it is…"

From the depths of his truck
Vincent proclaimed
"Poetry is the language of the soul"

A RAINY SUNDAY WITH MAX

That day was windy
So windy that the market was empty
I was out on the main street
Handing out damp flyers for my book
Laughing at myself
Laughing at this absurd situation

Max came to see me

He stayed there
In the cold
Just to keep me company
For friendship's sake
We talked a little
Then we went to the café
The warm café

He told me he had a dream
Of playing soccer on a professional team
He left Senegal
He and his family had to pay
4000 euros
His best friend sold his car
To help him out

In France his agent dropped him
He slept in the street
There were days when he didn't eat
He had hard times
For several months

Many people helped him
And now he's here
With me
In the café
He never doubted his talent

I saw in his eyes
Something we rarely see
A flame
Determination and craziness
Facing the immense wave of reality
And the immense wave of his dream

Outside
The wind blew
And the rain fell
But the flame never flickered
Not for one second

✲✲

THE WILD CHILD

At the market in Belvès
In the middle of the summer
I saw a couple of tourists with a child on a leash
A harness around his torso
The father was holding him tight
Pulling on the rope

A knife vendor and I looked at each other
We hesitated
Should we say something?

I'll always remember the father's expression
Running out of patience
And aggressive
And the child
Almost wild
In the crowd
Like a dog

⁎

DOG ON A CHAIN

At the Saint-Cyprien market
There was a dog
A basset hound
Low
Stocky
Floppy lips hanging all over the place
He was overexcited

His mistress held him by the chain around his neck
And beat him with the chain
To make him hold still
The dog wagged his tail
As the blows rained down

He adopted a 'good boy' attitude
Waiting for the storm to pass
Not understanding why he was being beaten

Maybe he was thinking
That some people need to vent their frustration
On chained up dogs
And that these kinds of people deserve
Like the rest of us
A little sympathy

Or maybe
The dog accepted his condition as a slave
Using love to get by

NINETEEN YEARS OLD

She was working at the stand next to mine
She talked to me about the Gilets Jaunes
As it happens she's one of them

She saw cops threatening civilians
She saw cops beating a doctor
Who was helping a Gilet Jaune

She told me about tear-gas hand grenades
Wounds
Insults
Crowd entrapment
Orders to kill
Cops disguised as vandals

She kept on saying
"People don't know what's going on"

This young woman is nineteen years old
And she's scared for her future

I don't know what to say to her
I don't have the courage to fight
Like she does
I don't even have the right to speak
For her cause
But what she told me left its mark
And I had to write about it

THE BAREFOOT GODDESS

With Vincent the second hand bookseller
We used to call her the Barefoot Goddess
She had short hair
Very short
You could see her scalp
A lovely round face
Always wearing a smile
She had that limpid and troubled look in her eyes
People get when they've suffered
And are now looking for peace

She was walking barefoot
And Vincent thought she was beautiful
He wrote a poem for her
And every Sunday
We waited
To give her the poem
But she didn't show up again

Every Sunday
We were wondering
If she was avoiding us on purpose
If she was playing with us
This goddess
And when we lost hope
She appeared

I gave her Vincent's poem
She read it
She smiled
She blushed
She started to glow
Like a divinity

I never saw Vincent so happy
He was looking at her
Like a child
With sparkling eyes

MONPAZIER

I don't know what happened
I was in Monpazier
The market was finishing
The village was yellowed with sunlight
It was hot and dry

When I started to pack up
I saw
Quite far off
A woman in a wheelchair
And a man next to her
Stroking her neck gently
As he walked

I don't know what came over me
It was so beautiful
That I felt awful
I felt lonely

***

MONTIGNAC CHAPEL

Yesterday
I was over there
For a Christmas market
A cold and damp November day
In a freezing chapel

All day long I waited
To sell a book
I hadn't sold one for a week
A week of doubts and questions
How long will I be able to keep going?

Still
I'm meeting fantastic people

A sweet young woman
Who talks to me about God and Archangels
With great tact

But also a wood turner
Who's proud to spend his life chilling out
After ten years in a Spanish desert

Night falls
And I still haven't sold a book
I wonder what I'm doing here
I'm cold
I'm tired

I'm reading a book about drugs

Suddenly
I see two flashes
Two kids running around
In the freezing chapel
They're right
They laugh shamelessly
Escapees from their mother's watch

The youngest
And craziest
Goes outside in the rain
And stares up
Amazed
Fascinated
Rain pouring down on his face
Then he comes back in and starts to run around again

I go to a responsible adult and whisper
"Apparently this child loves rain…"
His mother realizes what's going on
She sees this small innocent human being
Drenched from head to toe
Without the slightest shiver
He had run so much
Played so much
That he was gorged with summer sun

※

AFTER THE MARKET

Often
After the market
I play basketball
To clear my head

One day
Nathan came to play ball with me
Nathan is my neighbour
We live in the same social housing estate
He's thirteen I think

While shooting hoops
I ask him
"Isn't school a pain in the ass?"
And he replies
"I'd rather not think that, it would only make it worse"

We have a philosopher here
Between two shots
I ask
"What's your number one quality?"
Without thinking he replies
"Listening"

So
Impressed
I ponder on this word
In silence
After thinking for a while
A question arises
A question that has preoccupied me lately
"What's the secret of success?"
Throwing the ball in the air
Nathan declares
"Perseverance"

PEDRO AND THE BULL

From the top of the stairs
I can see Pedro at his stand
Talking to two kids
Not trying to sell them anything
Just enjoying telling a story

He brandishes a long hunting knife
And declaims dramatically
"That, my friend, is a blade
Used in Spain
For the corrida
When the bullfighter faces the bull head on"

Pedro catches me smiling
But he remains untroubled
Holding his audience spellbound
The knife high in his left hand
The kid's eyes glued to him
They are in the arena
They see the bull
They see Pedro facing the beast

"And then
The bullfighter shouts
Come on bull! Venga toro! Venga!
The bull charges to skewer him
But at the very last second
Ka-pow!
Between the eyes!"
Pedro swings his sword
Slicing the air
Felling the imaginary bull
With his bare hands
Right in front of the stunned kids

CHRISTIAN

Christian sells jewellery
He's about sixty
A hefty and bald man
With a deep voice
He's what you'd call a character
Criticizing the whole world
With humour and wit
Mixing fine words with
Obscenities

But when a customer stops by
He turns into a gazelle tamer
Treading softly
So as not to frighten away the shy animal

His mellow voice
Makes the rest of the market disappear
As he leads the woman into
His kingdom of mirrors and jewels

Adeptly
Christian clips a necklace onto her
Attentive and smooth
He embellishes the shy animal
Who goes off
Light hearted

Still under the charm of his melodious voice

Then Christian
Turns back to me
Same old prick
Spitting brashly
On the face of the world

DAVID — EXODUS

I'd never met a *manouche* before
One day I was setting up in Le Bugue next to David
He sells crêpes
He's extremely kind
Which is often the case with *manouches*
Who tend to fight their bad reputation
With thoughtfulness and courtesy

David tells me his people come from Rajasthan
They were driven out of that kingdom
A long time ago
They travelled across half the world
Via Mongolia
Russia
Central and Western Europe

In every country
They picked up words
Expressions
Mapping their exodus
In their language

※

DAVID — PLANE TREES AND PINES

David told me he grew up in a family of carnies
Every week he went to school in a different town

One day we talked about trees
I said I especially liked plane trees
Even if they are very common
He replied
"You know
I like plane trees too
I'm gonna tell you why
When I was a child
Every time we went to a new village
We set up the attractions in the main square
Usually there were plane trees
And we used to carve our names
And messages of love
In the bark

Often David stares at a far-off horizon
He seems nostalgic
The day we talked about trees
He whispered
"You know
All I need to be happy
Is a tiny spot by the ocean
My family
My friends
And pine trees"

AMBRE

I was setting up my stand at Spoonfest
At Copeaux Cabana
And talking to Johanna
She had a little girl with her
Seven or eight years old
She seemed normal
Just a bit restless
Wearing headphones

Her name was Ambre

I saw them again
And found out that Ambre has a degenerative disease
Her brain
Is slowly
Losing its abilities
She emits strange sounds
Like an underwater creature
Lost in the ocean

She talks with her hands
She makes up her own language
She hits things
To make the world resound
Like a musician
Discovering a new instrument
With clenched fingers

Sometimes she rolls on the ground
Then bangs her forehead with her clumsy fist
To get her brain to work
And then a serious expression comes over her
And her eyes reflect something
Far too deep
For us to understand

Sometimes she breaks into wild laughter
And runs into the streets
Towards cars and death
As if she were challenging
An invisible force

Once
I tried to be polite and said
"Hi!"
Her mother asked "Did you say hello, Ambre?"
The little girl didn't say a word
She didn't even look at me

Then I waved
Like you'd wave to somebody on the other shore of life
I stretched out my hand
Trying to speak her language
And
Without looking at me

She touched the centre of my palm
With her finger

I guess that meant "hi!"

THE DANCER

Heat wave
Disastrous book fair
Nobody came for the authors
I sold nothing that day

On the other hand
I met Pierre, Fabrice and Elise
They invited me to come with them
They rescued me

We left in a car together
As if we'd known each other forever
Elise drove very fast
Music at top volume
Windows open
We arrived at the house of a guy I didn't know
He had a swimming pool

I said to myself this is an incredible day
Everything was unexpected
The way we met
The car ride
The music
The garden
The discussions
The cool shade of the cabin

And especially
Especially
Elise dancing
Barefoot
On the edge of the pool

JACQUOU

To help me sell books
Pedro comes up to passers-by
He hails them
"Do you know the ancestor of Jacquou Le Croquant?"
People look at him with a strange expression
Without letting them answer
He points at me and says
Dramatically
"It's him!"

Pedro calls me Jacquou
'Cause he doesn't know my name

He often repeats
"Don't forget me, Jacquou
When you're famous and get to be on television
Don't forget me"
Then I reply
"I'll tell them that I made it thanks to you
I'll tell them: Pedro taught me everything"

One day
He came to see me and whispered
"This morning
Jacquou
I prayed for you

I prayed to the Lord
I asked him to help you
I'm telling you
You're gonna sell a lot of books today"

I don't know if the Lord exists
Or if it's Pedro's talent
But every time we were at the same market
I did pretty well

CAR CHASE

R. helped me build my cart
We were in his garden
Talking
He told me that the police had come to question him
That very morning
I asked him why
And he told me

"I was on the phone with my ex
Telling her that I was suffering
That I missed her

She laughed
'You're not going to start crying again!'
And in the background
Her new guy laughed as well

A few days later
I saw the guy who'd made fun of me
Driving by
I hung a u-turn and followed him
Rammed him
And bashed in his car
And when he got out
I slapped him a few times
To warm-up his ears"

Now R. is going to be judged
He's going to pay for his outburst
But if he had to do it again
He would

While we were working on the cart
I secretly admired this nutcase
Who won't have anyone mocking his tears

MAMMY JOSÉPI

It was a damp December Saturday
In Sarlat
A little lady appeared in the market
Wearing a rain jacket
A woolly hat pulled down over her glasses
A hunched back

All of a sudden
She shouts at the top of her voice
"You can all go home now
Mammy Josépi's gonna steal the show!
Soap!
Detergent!
Ladies and Gentlemen
Everything must go
The best detergent in the world is mine
I made it this morning!"

She's hawking
A few bits of soap
And homemade detergent in a can
Set on a miserable table

Right away
Two people stop
She babbles

Argues
And sells them her homemade stuff
At an unbeatable price

"I'm a Zen monk and a samurai
My psychoanalyst told me so"
She claims to have five lovers in Sarlat
Tonight she's going to improvise on stage
At the Lune-Poivre bar
Then she's going to party in a club
God knows where
She starts to dance and scream
"Mammy Josépi is here ladies and gentleman
It's now or never!
The best detergent in the world!"

It rains on the crowd
And the soap is melting away
She's chain smoking
She hides her true face

I ask her
"Would you like to sell books?
I'd give you a commission"
She comes closer
Takes a look at my book
Suddenly the cops arrive
She checks them out with the furtive glance

Of a Zen monk samurai
Then screams
"Oh I had a lover in the police
As a matter of fact
Blue's always been my favourite colour"
And she dances after them
  Trying to sell them soap and the best detergent in the world

THE HOOKER

Often the guys at the market
Go on and on
"Thirty years I've been a hooker
I've never seen this
Nobody buys anything anymore"

Sometimes I get bitter too
I see myself
Standing in the street
In the rain
Pushing the cart
Which is now soaking wet
Under a small umbrella
Hookering
Starving
Handing out flyers
Shivering
Stuttering
"Do you want a summary?"
To people who obviously don't give a fuck

All this to sell one book…

Sometimes
It's so ludicrous
It makes me laugh
And then I realize
I'm exactly where I belong
And this is what it means to be free

FOR CÉCILE

Hundreds of people as far as the eye can see
An old lady
And her teenage grand-daughter
Stop by my stand

I show them the poem
"In Monpazier"
I don't know why
Normally
I never choose that one
It's a bit sad

The old lady reads it
I see her eyes getting misty
Above her mask
"That's the way it was with my husband"
She says

The crowd disappears
From around us

She buys the book
I write a dedication
For Cécile
Thank you for shared emotion
It's the first thing that crossed my mind

Reading this
Her eyes cloud up again
She whispers
"Yes
Shared emotion
That's what it is"

The young girl wraps her arm around
The old lady's shoulder
As they leave
Swallowed back into the noise
And the heat of the market

THE BLIND LADY

The little ageless woman
Walked slowly
Through the Bugue market
With a cane
Head hanging low
Bulbous peasant nose
And short dark hair

Blank eyes staring ahead
Ears wide open
Moving carefully between the stands

It was a windy day
With fat grey clouds
She couldn't see
But perhaps could feel

She tapped obstacles with her cane
Heading towards the square
We all watched
She must have heard us watching

Several times I wanted to give her a hand
She was doing fine on her own
But every move was difficult

Her handbag slid down her arm
Entangled with a basket and cane
She stopped to put it back in place

It took forever

She reached the stand she was looking for
But the person she wanted to talk to wasn't there

So she walked back
Adrift
Like an island
Alone
Mysterious
And dignified
Touching the world with the tip of her cane

THE DOG

When I get lonely
I go to see The Dog
My friend Charley's
Brown Labrador

The Dog is always glad to see me
He runs towards me rejoicing
Bouncing left and right
Wagging his tail fanatically
With an infinite supply of energy

It looks like he's showing me how to live
It looks like he's talking
It looks like he's saying
"Only zeal matters"

On the other hand
The Dog also likes to eat shit
But after all
To each his own
Who am I to judge?

His eyes never lie
His eyes are full of love
For me or for shit
It doesn't make any difference
It's the fervour that counts

THE PIANIST

Christian is a mentally handicapped old man
Who lives in a retirement home

He's scary looking
And tires everyone out
Running around
And giggling

Christian is frenzy embodied

Often
He will stare at you
And with a frightening expression
Talk fast

Every time I see him
He makes me laugh
He runs towards me
With his crazy eyes
A hand outstretched
To greet me

 - NICE WEATHER, RIGHT? NICE WEATHER!
WHERE YOU GOING? HI! YOU OK?
 - I'm all right Christian. How about you?
 - WHO?

- You, Christian, you're all right?
- HE HE! WHERE YOU GOING, HUH? WHERE YOU GOING?
- I'm going to play the piano, you wanna come?

In the room
Cranky old people groan
"For Christ sake, make him shut up!"

Christian and I
Go to the auditorium
Where there's an old out-of-tune piano

Like a child
He bangs on all the keys
Laughing his head off
Then I start to play
Low notes
With my left hand

His eyes freeze
I tell him
"Press here!"
Pointing at some black keys
- HERE?
- Yes, here.
- HERE?

- Yes
And he starts to play
Standing
Along with me
Without hesitation
He hits two notes
With both hands out flat
He's not laughing anymore
He grinds his teeth
Beats the rhythm with his foot
His entire being focuses
On this strange music
As if nothing else existed

PEDRO PLAYING GUITAR

Like most French gypsies
Pedro is evangelist
The first time we talked
He told me God had cured his throat cancer

Pedro has lived a million lives
One of them was devoted to Catalan rhumba
An offshoot of flamenco
He played guitar and sang at the top of his lungs
Outside restaurants in Sarlat
He made thousands of francs every night
Those were the days…

Then he met Jesus
And gave up rhumba
Now he mostly sings evangelist hymns
Composed by gypsies

One Wednesday morning
I brought my guitar
To hear him play
He began singing glory to the Lord
Another voice arose
A guy selling mattresses
A few feet away
Who knew the words by heart

They got together
They smiled at each other
And bathed in the magnificent July sunlight
Sang their hymns
About God and Jesus and the Virgin
People passing by were ill at ease

JOKO

I've only seen Joko twice
Both times he made an impression on me

Joko barely knew his father
Left home at seventeen
Destination Saint-Raphaël
Hung out with the wrong crowd
Drugs
The street
Violence
Begged in the Paris metro
Dealt drugs for years
Learned how to pick locks
And never got caught

When I met him
He was about to get a new set of teeth
Because his ex
A junky punk
Had attacked him
But he didn't hold it against her

Joko talked a lot
He had no regrets
He even sang a song to me

Written for another ex-girlfriend
About how life is hard
But there's always a way

Six months later I saw him again
In the middle of summer
At the Sainte-Alvère market
He told me more about his life
He told me about the memory gaps he has
Since he accidentally overdosed
On hallucinogens

Such a chaotic life and absence of bitterness
Left me dumbfounded
It made me wonder what was his secret
This is what he said
"Often
People talk about spirituality
You should do this or that
Complicated stuff
But what works for me
Is walking in the woods
And thanking
Everything around me"

✱

TELEPATHIST

I remember
At the very beginning
When I worked with Vincent
At the Buisson market
A lady bought five of my books in one go

She was quite a tall woman
Imposing
She spoke slowly with a German accent
And had a strange look in her eyes

I asked
"What do you do?"
She hesitated
But eventually replied
"I cure animals
I talk with them
Through telepathy"

She smiled at me with a bizarre look
She wasn't fooling around

※

FLAMENCO

I don't know his first name
We'd met often in Montignac
We talked about literature
He's a guitarist in a band that's pretty well-known around here

One day he brought his red-stringed guitar
The market was empty
Very few stands
No customers
The sky was a low
Grey confusion of clouds

He played flamenco
Notes overlapping notes
Bouncing off the white church walls in front of us

The rhythm was galloping
Rearing up
Bursting through the greyness
With invisible rays

In his guitar
There was something
That made the heart weep
And rejoice as well

GURDJIEFF

I met in Lalinde
An unbelievable character
A man about seventy
Crippled
Lame
In rags
Greasy hair
Long fingernails
He smelled of urine
His nose was caked with blood

A man in bad shape
Very bad shape

He spoke to me about the Gurdjieff scale
Mumbling obscure and
Incomprehensible nonsense

But his eyes glimmered softly
As if they could embrace your whole soul
In one look

※

JENNY

It was Sunday morning
Orian the wandering baker
Introduced me to Jenny
A young woman with sunglasses
Sitting on the steps outside a shop
She wrote her address on a piece of paper for me
I noticed something weird about her middle finger
Tactlessly
I asked
"What happened to you?"

A machine for sorting walnuts
Snatched the finger
For months it hung by a thread
For months it kept on bleeding
For months she thought she would lose it
Eventually
After several operations
It looked like a human finger again

Jenny, Orian and I
Stayed together after the market
We went to the river
Sometimes we talked about the finger
I had the feeling she thought of it
As a person

Discretely
I watched her dip half her hand
Into the river
All her other fingers
Took care of the one in the middle
Carefully and lovingly
Like brothers and sisters might do
With a newborn child

BERTOLUCCI

At the outskirts of the village
There is a horse
Alone in a paddock

When it rains
When it's windy
When it freezes
The horse circles slowly
Locked in

His lips level with the ground
Picking up a few twigs

I call him Bertolucci
God knows why
I try to coax him
With carrots
And fistfuls of grass

In spite of my offerings
Old Berto doesn't want to be patted
Perhaps he holds a grudge against humans
I can understand

When I arrive at the paddock
I shout "Bertoluuuuuuuucci!"
He recognizes the call
And heads towards me
To get his share of carrots
And grass

He never runs
Never neighs
He just looks straight at me
With his sorrowful eyes

One cold day
I sat on a stone to admire him
He was circling as usual
Then he stopped in the middle of the paddock
Stared at the hills
Far away
And…
Had an erection
Yes
He had a hard-on
As only horses can:
Nobly

After a moment of surprise
I said to myself
Maybe he's a poet horse
And hills remind him of a rump

Maybe he met a mare
A long time ago
And misses her

I don't know why fate wanted me to be here
At this very moment
I don't know what to make of it
All I can say is this
No one has ever expressed solitude
With more eloquence than Bertolucci

LE BERCAIL (THE FOLD)

Le Bercail is a former monastery
Converted into a home for mentally handicapped adults
I'd offered to spend an evening there
To practice reading in public
I expected five or six people would show up

Forty came

Forty mentally handicapped adults
Sitting in a half circle around me
Listening to excerpts from *Le Petit Prince*

I began reading
With a bit of anxiety

They were all hanging on my every word
Except for one woman who talked non-stop
She couldn't care less about the story

It was dark outside
The room was filled with an extremely strange atmosphere
There were all sorts of faces and expressions
All sorts of mental deficiencies
What did they understand?

What did they feel?
I didn't have a clue
But I kept on reading the best I could
Amidst forty pairs of eyes

At the end of the reading
They gave me a good round of applause
It warmed my heart
Without entirely dissolving my anxiety

When it was quiet again
A handicapped woman asked me
With disarming naïveté
"But how come you know how to read?"
I replied without thinking
"Because I learned"

She was staggered

Knowing how to read
Learning
Of the whole evening, that's what she found extraordinary
And when you think about it
It is extraordinary

⁎⁎⁎

If you wish to share your impressions you can contact me at + 33 768 57 70 08 / finoki@yahoo.fr